The Piano Owner's Manual

by
Steven R. Snyder

Published by
SRS Co.
2554 Lincoln Blvd.
Suite 160
Marina del Rey, CA 90291

Illustrations by Steven R. Snyder

Cover by Andreas M. Gross

ISBN: 0-9610766-0-7

Printed in the United States of America

Anything of value in life is rarely the effort of a single individual and this book is no exception.

I would like to thank my wife Patricia for her help and guidance. Without her love and assistance this project would not have been possible.

I would also like to thank my editors, Marion Morgan and Marion Schmidt for their enthusiastic support, and my father, Robert E. Snyder, for his inspired contributions. And last but not least, my thanks to Christopher Peto for proofing.

TABLE OF CONTENTS

ILLUSTRATIONS

INTRODUCTION

Having been a piano tuner-technician for more than ten years, I have gained most of my experience servicing pianos directly in the customer's home. I have made tuning and repair service calls for many of the well-known piano companies in Boston, New York City, and Los Angeles. I have also tuned for recording and rehearsal studios and for many popular artists.

The Piano Owner's Manual is not a technician's handbook. Designed for piano owners, it is my response to the many questions asked me regarding pianos. My extensive work in homes and studios has given me a unique opportunity to talk with pianists of every skill level. From beginner to accomplished artist, most people want to know many of the same things.

How to clean a piano without damaging it, how to solve simple repair problems, and how to understand the piano as an instrument are some of the basic areas of concern for most piano owners. An artist wants to understand how the piano functions in order to gain the greatest range of expression from his instrument, while the piano owner in general wants to protect his investment. Both are searching for the same information regarding pianos.

Through proper cleaning, moth protection, correct piano placement, climate control, and minor adjustments, one can virtually eliminate costly repairs and enjoy thousands of hours of trouble-free music. A piano is one of the most esthetically beautiful, sensitive, yet durable instruments ever invented. When maintained properly, a piano can last over one hundred years! Pianos bring joy and fulfillment to millions of people. They are something worth preserving.

1
Piano Types

1.1 CONSOLE PIANO

A *console piano* is a vertical piano. A *vertical piano* is any piano with·the strings in a vertical position, in contrast to a *grand piano,* which has strings in a horizontal position. Vertical pianos come in three sizes: *Spinet, console,* and *upright.* The size of a vertical piano is measured from the floor to the top of the lid.

The easiest way to identify a console piano is to measure it. The smallest vertical piano is known as the spinet, and measures about forty inches or less. The *studio upright* or console, as it is better known, ranges from forty inches to forty-nine inches tall. The largest of the three vertical pianos is the upright, which measures about fifty inches or more (see Plate No. 3).

Another identifying feature of the console piano is the location of the piano *action.* A piano action is that part of the piano that transfers the striking force from the key to the string. As shown in Plate No. 6, the console piano action sits directly on top of the keys.

In the console piano illustration, the most commonly referred to cabinet parts are labeled. It is much easier to discuss replacements or repairs if you know the names of the parts, and knowing them also brings you a step closer to understanding your piano.

CONSOLE PIANO

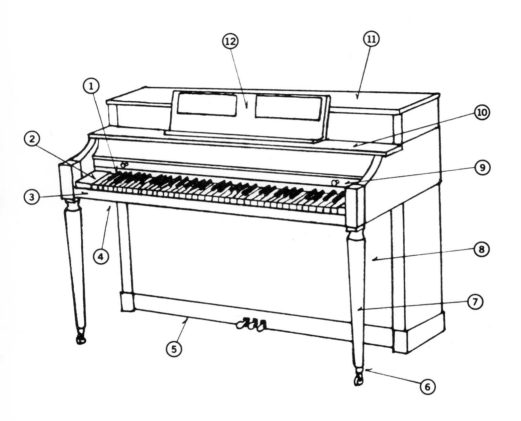

① FALL STRIP	⑤ BOTTOM BOARD	⑨ FALLBOARD
② KEYBLOCK	⑥ CASTER	⑩ MUSIC SHELF
③ KEYSLIP	⑦ LEG	⑪ LID
④ KEYBED	⑧ LOWER FRAME	⑫ MUSIC DESK

Plate No. 1

1.2 SPINET PIANO

The spinet piano is the smallest of the vertical pianos. It has what is known as a drop action which means that the action is below the level of the keys. For a detailed view of a spinet piano action, see Plate No. 16.

In outward appearance, the spinet piano is much like the console piano because many spinets and consoles are similar in height. The major difference between the two pianos is the location of the action within the piano case. In the spinet piano illustration, the *music shelf, fallboard,* and *lower frame* have been removed to give a clear view of the drop action as it is placed in the piano.

The action is supported by a long block of wood (1) inside the piano. Since the piano action is below the keys (2), *drop stickers* or *lifter wires* (3) are used to attach the keys to the action. The spinet's drop stickers make it very difficult for piano technicians to service spinet pianos because it is difficult to reach in between the stickers to repair a faulty action part. When a repair is necessary, the technician must remove the entire action before attempting the repair. Removal of a spinet action can be very complicated and often means higher repair costs to the spinet piano owner.

SPINET PIANO

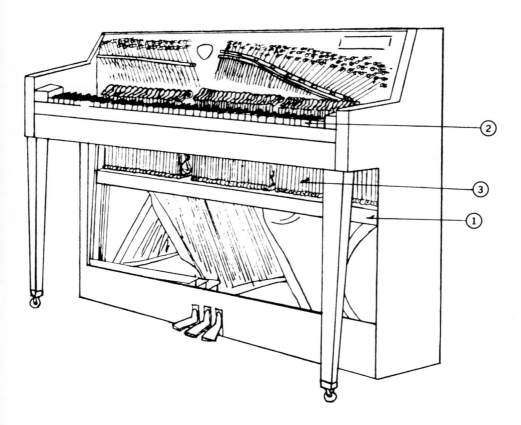

① SUPPORT BLOCK

② KEYS

③ DROP STICKERS

Plate No. 2

1.3 UPRIGHT PIANO

The tallest of the vertical pianos is the upright piano. Its added height gives it a richness and tonal quality comparable to those of many grands. The illustration of a typical modern upright piano shows the difference in size among upright, console, and spinet pianos. All pianos are basically the same width if they have eighty-eight keys. The taller the piano, the longer the strings and the richer the tone.

The location of the action is the unique feature that distinguishes upright pianos from spinets and consoles. The upright piano action is located above the piano keys and rests on *stickers.* Stickers are usually made of wood and are connected to the action, rather than being attached to the keys as they are in spinet pianos. Stickers vary in length proportionally with the height of the piano. For a detailed illustration and location of a sticker, refer to Plate No. 7.

MODERN UPRIGHT PIANO

AVERAGE HEIGHTS OF VERTICAL PIANOS

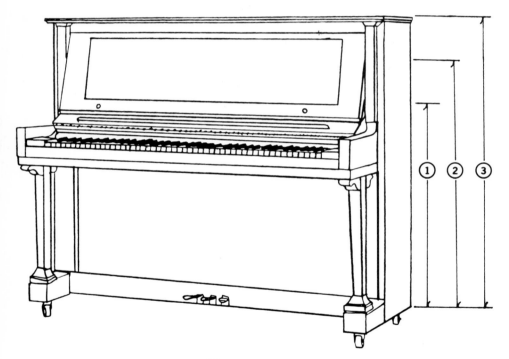

① SPINET

② CONSOLE

③ UPRIGHT

Plate No. 3

1.4   GRAND PIANO

A grand piano is a piano with its strings in a horizontal position. The most important feature of the grand piano cabinet is the length, measured horizontally from the *keyslip* (5) to the back edge of the *lid* (6). Grand pianos are built in progressive sizes from four feet eleven inches to over nine feet. Each size is about one inch longer than the next. Many of these piano sizes are given different names.

The smallest grand, usually about four feet eleven inches, is called the Apartment Grand. The Baby Grand measures five feet eight inches. The Living Room Grand is five feet ten inches long. The Professional Grand is six feet to six feet eight inches long and is the one most often used in recording studios. Pianos ranging from six feet eight inches to six feet ten inches are given the general name of Music Room Grand. The Semi Concert Grand measures seven feet four inches, and the Concert Grand measures eight feet eleven inches and longer. The added length given to Concert Grands increases the tonal quality, volume, and depth of expression needed to project throughout large concert halls.

GRAND PIANO

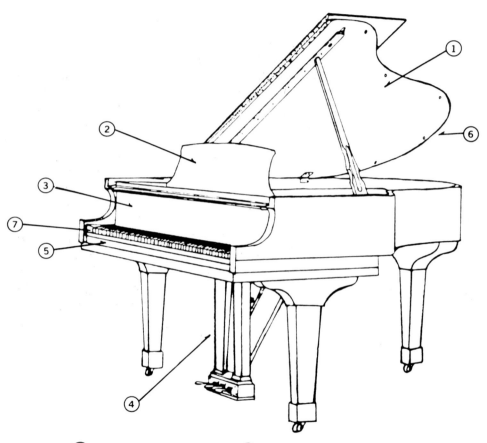

① LID   ④ LYRE

② MUSIC DESK   ⑤ KEYSLIP

③ FALLBOARD   ⑥ BACK EDGE OF LID

                 ⑦ KEYBLOCK

Plate No. 4

1.5 GRAND PIANO ACTION

The piano action, that part of the piano that transfers the striking force from the key to the string, is the heart of every piano. It looks complicated, but it is not as complex as it seems. My purpose here is to familiarize you with the basic parts of the action so that you are able to identify these parts in your piano.

If you look at the *Grand Piano Action* illustration, you will see how a piano works. You strike the *key* (5) to play a note. The piano key is a solid piece of soft wood with the striking surface covered by plastic, or sometimes ivory. When the key is struck, it contacts the *wippen assembly* (4). The wippen makes the *hammer* (3) rise up to strike the *string* (1). While the key is depressed, the *damper* (2) is lifted off the string, and the note continues to ring until the key is released.

The parts shown in black (with the exception of the piano key) are felt. The hammer is also felt, glued and tacked onto a wood molding. Felt piano parts are subject to attack by moths. As you can imagine, substantial damage can be done if moths are allowed to eat the felts. I will go further into moth protection in Section 5.

The string is wound around the *tuning pin* (8), which is driven into the *pinblock* (6). The pinblock is a laminated block of wood, attached underneath the *plate* (7). Laminated wood pinblocks have superior strength compared to solid wood pinblocks, and the laminations help to keep the tuning pins tight for a longer period of time. The importance of tight tuning pins is discussed in further detail in the section *Why Does A Piano Need To Be Tuned?*

GRAND PIANO ACTION

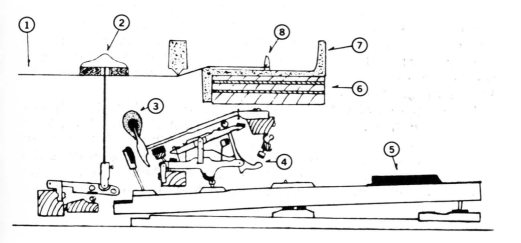

①STRING   ⑤KEY

②DAMPER   ⑥PINBLOCK

③HAMMER   ⑦PLATE

④WIPPEN   ⑧TUNING PIN
   ASSEMBLY

Plate No. 5

1.6 CONSOLE PIANO ACTION

The action of all vertical pianos functions basically like that of the console piano. Console and upright pianos have the piano action sitting on top of the keys, with the hammers standing in an upright position. The action of the hammer striking the string is on the horizontal plane. On a grand piano, the hammers are lying down and strike the string on the vertical plane, allowing gravity to return a hammer to its original position. Grand actions repeat faster than verticals because of this design.

Although many of the basic parts in the console piano action differ from those of spinets and uprights, they generally serve the same purpose. The key (5) is depressed, contacting the wippen assembly (4). This forces the *jack* (7) to push up the hammer butt, and the hammer (3) strikes the string (1). When the key is released, the escapement (consisting of a *spring* and *bridle strap*) pulls the hammer back to its original position.

The escapement action parts become worn rather quickly and need replacement sooner than the other action parts. If a part is worn or out of adjustment, the hammer may "bobble" against the string when played. Usually, replacement of the bridle straps and a few minor adjustments will correct the problem. It is a simple procedure but should be done by a qualified piano technician.

CONSOLE PIANO ACTION

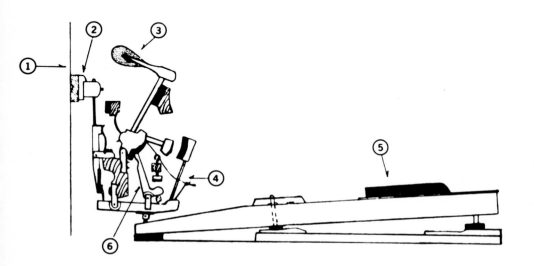

①STRING

②DAMPER

③HAMMER

④WIPPEN ASSEMBLY

⑤KEY

⑥JACK

Plate No. 6

1.7 UPRIGHT PIANO ACTION

The upright piano action works the same way as the console piano action with one major difference, the sticker (1). The sticker sits on the key, and when the key is depressed, the force is transferred to the sticker, which is attached to the wippen assembly (5). The wippen then forces the hammer (4) to strike the string (2).

UPRIGHT PIANO ACTION

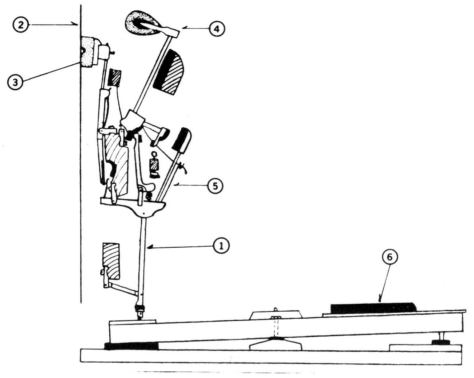

①STICKER

②STRING

③DAMPER

④HAMMER

⑤WIPPEN ASSEMBLY

⑥KEY

Plate No. 7

21

2

How To Clean A Piano Properly

2.1 WHY CLEAN A PIANO?

A general cleaning will enhance the appearance of your piano and prevent many repair problems in the future. Sometimes a good thorough cleaning is all that is needed to improve a piano's performance. Of course, you can pay a piano technician to clean your piano, but you can also clean it yourself. If you own a grand piano, see the sections on *Cleaning — Strings* and *Cleaning — Soundboard.* If you own a vertical piano, first check the *bottom board* (2) of your piano by removing the *lower frame,* and examine the *trapwork* (1) area. The vertical piano's bottom board supports the pedals and the trapwork, which is located at the bottom of the piano.

VERTICAL PIANO WITH LOWER FRAME REMOVED

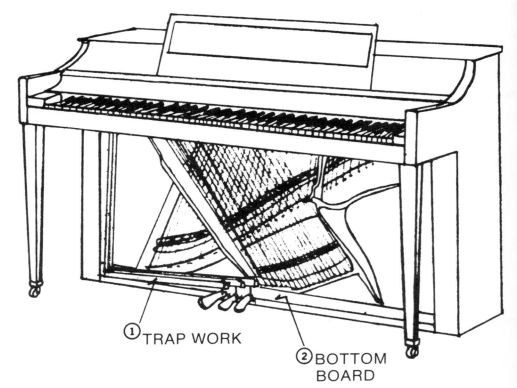

①TRAP WORK

②BOTTOM BOARD

Plate No. 8

If this is the first time that you have cleaned your piano, you may have to vacuum the trapwork area. However, afterwards a good cleaning with a damp cloth should be all that is necessary. If you live in the country or near wildlife, this is an essential area for you to clean and check regularly, or you could be in for a surprise.

Some of the older homes in New England contain the most beautiful and ornately carved upright pianos in the world today. The types of wood used and the craftsmanship that created these pianos place them in a class by themselves. Longstanding testimonials to an age past, these magnificent old pianos have been, more often than not, neglected for years.

I received a call about "squeaking" in just such a piano. Assuming the problem to be the pedals, I made sure to pack my oil and powdered graphite, the lubricants most commonly used to remedy this condition. Armed with my cures, I arrived at a lovely New England home. The owner, an elderly lady, directed me to the piano. Her granddaughter had an interest in studying piano and had begun taking lessons a few weeks before. The woman explained that the squeaking occured when her granddaughter practiced and that this was distracting to the little girl.

When I checked the tuning of the piano, it was obvious that it hadn't been touched for generations, and a lot of work was required to get it into reasonable shape. It never ceases to amaze me that people can play pianos so out of tune without feeling discomfort. Before discussing tuning with the owner, I wanted to discover the cause of the squeaking. I checked each pedal numerous times without playing the piano. Squeaks can usually be identified by just working the pedals in this manner. There were no squeaks.

This has happened often. I receive a call or complaint about a malfunction in a customer's piano, but when I arrive and check the instrument, everything seems to be working fine. As soon as I leave, the problem seems to come back again. I haven't quite figured out whether this is my good fortune or the owner's bad luck. Consequently, I've learned to check problems thoroughly.

After telling the owner that the piano seemed to work fine and shrugging my shoulders, I removed the lower frame. To my surprise, there on the bottom board, to the right of the pedals, I discovered a little nest! Three little grey squirrels were curled up asleep, but the mother was nowhere to be seen. When the owner of the piano saw the squirrel's nest, she screamed so loudly that she nearly shook the house and I almost dropped the lower frame on my foot.

After things calmed down a bit, I carefully removed the nest, and the scared little animals cried when they were awakened. We had discovered the squeak. I found a home for the squirrels outside, repaired the neglected piano, and gave it a good cleaning.

The owner's granddaughter has long since moved away, but the owner cleans her piano frequently. So again, if you live in the country or near wildlife, the bottom board and trapwork area are essential spots for you to check and clean regularly. Little squirrels, mice, and the like enjoy building their nests here. Keep it clean!

2.2 CLEANING SOLUTIONS

The question most frequently asked by piano owners is, "What do I clean my piano with?" There are several options available. The easiest, also the least effective, is a cloth slightly dampened with water. This can be used to dust the piano case, plate, and other areas where daily dust accumulates. Remember that piano strings are made of steel. Do not use a damp cloth on any steel parts, or they will rust.

A damp cloth is really adequate for daily or weekly dustings. However, to clean a piano thoroughly, which I discuss in detail further on, more effective cleaning solutions are recommended. A cleaning solution popular with many piano technicians is two tablespoons of vinegar mixed well with one gallon of warm water. A mild solution of Ivory soap or any liquid ammonia detergent diluted with water can also be used. Spray cleaners are all right to use, but should be applied with a damp cloth rather than sprayed directly on to the piano. This method is the least complicated way of getting tough cleaning jobs done, but, here again, avoid getting any liquid or dampness on the strings.

2.3 CLEANING — KEYS

Since the wild-life conservation act was passed to protect the elephant population, it is illegal to manufacture pianos with ivory keys in the United States. Therefore, piano manufacturers have switched to plastic and some plastic key tops even have grains in them to simulate the look and feel of the old ivory keys.

Many older pianos still in active use today do, however, have ivory key tops. One such piano was a spinet that I tuned recently. The owner said that she had cleaned the keys just before I arrived. She was a very conscientious lady who was obviously proud of her piano.

I was pleased to see a person so concerned about maintaining her piano, which appeared to be in excellent condition. I started to play the piano to check its tune and quickly jerked my hands away. I had experienced a queer sensation that made my flesh crawl. Then I noticed a sour smell and the dull, scummy film on the piano keys. The woman observed my reaction with surprise. When I asked what she had so painstakingly cleaned her keys with, she explained that she always cleaned them with milk!

If you own a piano that has genuine ivory keys, please do not clean them with milk. The misconception that ivory piano keys must be cleaned this way has circulated long enough! It is my hope that this old rumor will be stopped here, once and for all. The only thing that milk does to ivory keys is make them stink and coat them with a sticky scum most unpleasant to feel. Please do not put milk on your piano keys.

The best way to clean piano keys, both white and black, ivory and plastic, is with any of the cleaning solutions mentioned in the previous section. You must be careful not to use too much cleanser or water. Excess moisture could be harmful to the wood and felt bushings that the keys are mounted upon. Just a light touch of your cleaning solution applied to a damp cloth will clean the keys just fine. Be sure to dry the keys thoroughly after cleaning to avoid moisture damage and to give them that well polished look. And keep in mind that cleaning jobs will be simpler if you wash your hands before playing the piano.

2.4 CLEANING — CASE

A *piano case* (the exterior body of the piano) should be cleaned in the same way you would clean any fine piece of furniture, with a few exceptions. I recommend that you never use any type of aerosol furniture polish or, for that matter, any polish containing alcohol on your piano, as these will damage the finish. It is best to clean the case with a damp cloth or the water-vinegar solution mentioned earlier.

After cleaning the case, the next step is to wax and polish it. Furniture paste wax is the best wax to use on a piano case. A good polishing will result in a glossy finish and will properly condition the wood. It will also help ensure your piano's long life and preserve its value.

For the piano pedals and brass hinges, any good quality brass cleaner will do the job just fine. Remember to follow the directions when using a brass cleaner. This will produce the optimum results and make the brass sparkle like new.

2.5 CLEANING — STRINGS

Piano strings are made of steel and are sometimes referred to as piano wire or music wire. Strings vary greatly in diameter (thickness) and length. The strings on a vertical piano are more protected from the environment than the strings on a grand piano. Vertical piano strings, therefore, require less cleaning. To look at the strings on a vertical piano, you lift the lid and remove the music shelf (see Plate No. 1). This gives you a good view of the tuning pins and the top part of the strings. By removing the lower frame, you will be able to see the bottom part of the strings and decide whether they need cleaning. If they do, it is best to let a piano technician do the work, as it involves removing the action from the piano. For a grand piano, however, you can clean the strings yourself.

The condition of the piano strings will affect its tone. If you see that your piano's strings are rusty, or very dirty, it is time to clean them. The best procedure, especially on a grand piano, is to clean both the strings and the soundboard at the same time because the dirt and shavings from cleaning the strings will fall on the sound-board.

Do not use any cleanser when cleaning piano strings. Never use any oil on the strings or anywhere inside the piano. Oil will destroy a piano's tone and severely inhibit the piano's ability to stay in tune. I will explain later in the section on Protecting Your Investment how to prevent the formation of rust on the strings.

The best and easiest method of cleaning piano strings is rubbing them lightly with a fine grade of steel wool. Rub the strings back and forth, working out the rust until they shine. Use this method on bass strings, also. For cleaning the bass section, a heavier (coarser) grade of steel wool is recommended. Bass strings have a steel core with copper wound around it. The thick copper windings will rapidly disintegrate a fine grade of steel wool. As the note becomes lower, the copper windings become thicker, and the string increases in length for proper tone. Cleaning bass strings is a bit like polishing a copper penny. The more you rub, the more brilliantly they shine. Rubbing the strings back and forth disintegrates the steel wool, and on grand pianos these shavings fall on the soundboard. You can remove the shavings by blowing compressed air into the area or by cleaning the soundboard.

Compressed air or "shop" air, as it is often called, is available in professional workshops. It is very high pressure air suitable for a variety of applications and is generally not accessible to the piano owner. The exhaust from a vacuum cleaner is not as powerful as shop air and will not clean the soundboard sufficiently. The piano owner, therefore, should clean the soundboard by following the simple instructions given in the next section to achieve the best results. By properly cleaning the soundboard and the strings, the piano will look and sound its best.

2.6 CLEANING — SOUNDBOARD

The soundboard is the large board that forms the back of a vertical piano or the bottom of a grand piano. It is located behind the strings in vertical pianos, or under the strings in grands, and is attached to the plate. A soundboard is made of wood, usually spruce, and is about three-eighths of an inch thick. When a note is played, the soundboard vibrates and gives a more musical tone to the piano's voice.

The soundboard has a *crown* or gradual curve throughout the length of the piano. The crown may not be noticeable to the eye, but, if a piano soundboard has lost its crown, the ear can usually hear the difference. Pianos with flat soundboards have a dead sound and lack vibrance. Besides helping to produce a musical tone, the soundboard aids in resisting the tremendous downward pressure exerted by the piano strings. The vibration of the soundboard, coupled with the sound of the piano strings, then, creates the musical quality of tone that we hear when playing a note.

Soundboards on grand pianos collect a great deal of dirt through the years, especially if piano lids are left open. Grand pianos need cleaning far more often than vertical pianos because dust and dirt build up more easily on a horizontal surface than on a vertical surface. It is, therefore, prudent to keep the lid and fallboard on a grand piano closed when the piano is not in use. Vertical piano soundboards rarely need cleaning, but, as mentioned in the *Why Clean A Piano?* section, the bottom board should be checked regularly.

When cleaning a grand piano soundboard, technicians use a soundboard *steel*. This is a flat, flexible piece of steel with a hole in one end. This steel is generally about twenty four inches long and can be purchased very inexpensively at a piano store or from your piano technician. You must have this tool or a similar piece of spring steel in order to clean the soundboard. A vacuum cleaner will not reach down in between the strings to clean sufficiently. Compressed air blown across the area will remove debris and dust, but it will not remove stains or other types of ground-in dirt.

Dampen a cloth with any of the previously mentioned cleaning solutions. Pull a portion of the cloth through the hole in the soundboard steel. Securely tie a string about twelve inches long to the other end of the cloth. Start cleaning at the extreme right end of the piano (treble section) and clean to the lower left corner beyond the bass strings. Following this method will allow you to gather the accumulated dust and dirt at the unrestricted area of the sound-board, to the left of the bass section, and remove the debris easily.

Read the following instructions carefully and study the pictures to grasp the idea of the process.

CLEANING GRAND PIANO SOUNDBOARD — STEP 1

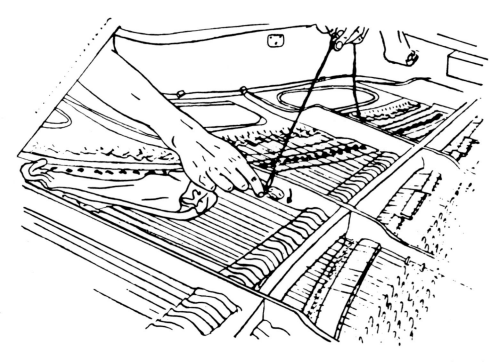

1) Insert the moist cloth, string end first, under the treble strings.

Plate No. 9

CLEANING GRAND PIANO SOUNDBOARD — STEP 2

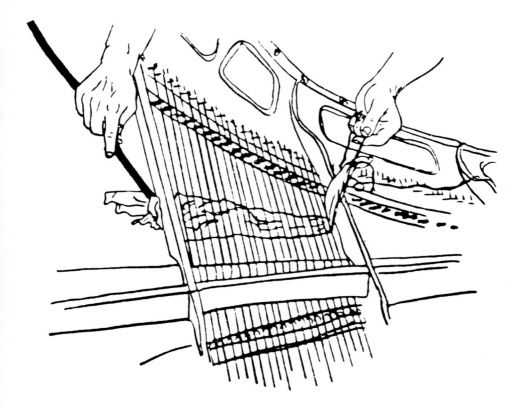

2) Work the cloth under the treble strings by pushing and pulling it back and forth with the soundboard steel. Once most of the cloth is under the treble strings, grab the string you tied to the cloth, and pull it up through the piano wire.

Plate No. 10

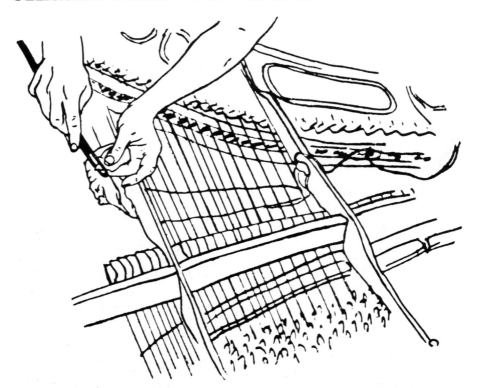

3) Insert the other end of the cloth through the hole in the soundboard steel.

Plate No. 11

Now you can push in one direction with the soundboard steel and
pull in the other direction with the string. By working the cloth back
and forth in this manner you will clean the soundboard.

When you have reached the point that you can't clean any further
with the present position of the soundboard steel, remove the cloth
from the piano. Rinse the cloth in the cleaning solution and insert
the whole arrangement as before. This time, start at the middle of the
piano and proceed to the bass section.

You will be amazed at how this cleaning will revitalize your piano.
When you have finished, the soundboard will look just like new, and
the piano will sound brighter, too. The technique of working the
cloth back and forth along the soundboard takes a little practice but
can be quickly mastered. A word of caution: always keep the cloth
between the soundboard steel and the soundboard itself, to avoid
unintentionally scratching the wood. Work all of the dirt and debris

to the extreme left side of the piano soundboard, where it can be easily removed with a moist cloth.

This is the method the professionals use, and now you can use it. The result will be a clean soundboard that will enhance the beauty of your piano for months to come. The best part is that you can do it yourself and save a lot of money in the process.

2.7 HOW OFTEN SHOULD A PIANO BE CLEANED?

A piano should be cleaned thoroughly once every two to three years. This amounts to a lot of cleaning, but it has its rewards. The useful life of a properly maintained piano is eighty to one hundred years before it needs a complete rebuilding.

If a grand piano is neglected and not cleaned at all, dirt and debris will fall on the bass strings and settle on the soundboard, deadening tone. The dirt will also find its way into the action, causing friction between finely fitted parts, gumming up the motion.

To avoid costly repair bills and, most important, to keep your piano in "mint" condition, clean it regularly. Regular and proper cleaning can make the difference between an increase and a decrease in your piano's value.

Most pianos, even small verticals, are rather large pieces of furniture and can collect a lot of dust and dirt. If not cleaned, a dirty piano can become an eyesore just like any other neglected piece of furniture. Most of my repairs begin with a complete cleaning of the instrument from top to bottom. Good piano technicians or mechanics will clean the item that they are working on as well as complete the repair.

The resale value of a piano (or anything, for that matter) can vary drastically between one that is clean and one that is not. A clean piano looks cared for. People who are planning to sell a piano should clean it first, in order to receive the best possible price for the instrument.

I was asked by a customer to appraise a piano, which was one of two for sale. Both were grands that had belonged to a famous concert artist who had recently died. The pianos had served as practice instruments for the artist when she was at home. My client was interested in the larger of the two. From this information, it sounded like a simple appraisal.

When I arrived , I thought that the home looked pretty small to have two grand pianos inside. I knocked on the door, and a very nice, elderly lady answered and saw me in. The sun was out, and it took my eyes a few moments to adjust to the dark interior of the house. The curtains were drawn, and there wasn't much light.

The living room contained enough furniture, plants, and paraphernalia to fill a mansion, but, sure enough, hidden under all of this were two grand pianos. They were stuffed into the far corner of the room, side by side, and virtually buried under an assortment of items.

When I finally dug out the piano that I was to appraise, I still needed more light to see the instrument clearly. After taking out my music lamp, turning it on, and setting it on the music shelf, I just about froze to the spot. There was the most beautiful rosewood grand I had ever seen. It was completely covered with dust and dirt, but I could tell that the finish was rosewood. The tone of the piano was exceptional, and the action was signed by the man who built it. That piano, made in nineteen hundred, was a rare gem dulled by the darkness of neglect. I was dumbfounded by its beauty.

My job was only to appraise the instrument for my client, and it was none of my business how much was being asked for it, but I couldn't resist inquiring about the price. The lady was selling that incredible rosewood piano for a small fraction of its original value. I told her that, if my client didn't buy the piano, I would!

Of course, my client did buy the piano. Happily, she contracted me to rebuild it. I refinished the rosewood case, repaired and regulated the action, and repinned and restrung the harp. My client now has a wonderful instrument. The piano is worth at least ten times what she paid for it.

When preparing to sell your piano, don't hide it in a corner or bury it under needless junk. A piano should be a display item, placed in an open area and appreciated for its beauty as well as its tone. The rosewood grand now stands in the center of my client's living room, which has a large picture window facing the street. All who pass by marvel at the beauty of this instrument. I suppose that this is justice done to a very special piano that had been neglected for so many years.

Your piano can have a similar effect on visitors. If you keep it clean and shiny, people will notice even the most humble instrument. Part of the joy of piano ownership is just looking at it in the home.

3

Minor Repairs

3.1 GENERAL

The repairs covered in this section pertain mainly to vertical pianos and can be accomplished without removing the piano's action. A willingness to get the job done and a keen eye are the most important tools you'll need.

To repair a grand piano, one must first remove the action and this can be a little tricky to do correctly. An inexperienced person is likely to depress some piano keys accidentally while sliding the action out of the piano. The depressed keys' hammers will break easily when they hit the pinblock. Hammer repairs require special tools. To avoid complications it is best to call a qualified piano tecnician for most grand piano repairs.

3.2 STICKY KEYS — GENERAL

There are five very common reasons for sticky keys. They are: 1) warped piano parts, 2) a foreign object inside the piano, 3) key bushings too tight, 4) one key interfering with the next, and 5) misalignment. Of course, an infinite number of possibilities could disrupt the proper action of a piano key, but usually the problem will turn out to be one of these five. All of these five can be easily remedied if approached in a systematic way.

First of all, carefully check the key or keys that are not functioning properly. If a careful examination of the outside of the piano reveals nothing out of the ordinary, such as a foreign object lodged between the keys, then a more critical look at the inside is necessary. At this time, you can usually narrow the cause down to one of the five possibilities given above, which are discussed in detail in this section. However, even sticky keys can have exotic or bizarre causes.

I remember receiving a call from a man who asked whether I could come for a tuning and repair of his grand piano. He said that he had been having some problems with a few sticky keys. Repairing grand pianos is usually more complex than repairing verticals because it involves removing the grand piano action, which is no small job in itself, but I agreed to take a look at his piano.

As I tried to play the middle section of the piano to check its tune, I realized that there were more than just a few sticky keys. Some notes sounded, but the keys stayed down; others played sluggishly, and still others didn't play at all. It seemed to me that I was looking at a piano that had every symptom in the book, and a few more! I began to realize thay my look at his piano could turn into a major rebuilding job, which might take months to complete.

I removed the fall strip and tried to dislodge the fallboard, the last part to go before sliding the action out of the piano, but it wouldn't budge. I checked the fallboard carefully and saw no reason why it shouldn't just come out, and so I forced it a little harder than I usually handle piano parts. The fallboard sprang out with a vengeance, propelled by a virtual flood of walnut shells, pecan shells, and acorns! I could hardly believe my eyes. It was like striking an oil well of nut shells.

Once this outpouring ceased, I surveyed the situation. The whole inside of the piano was full of shells. Every available nook and cranny had a shell stuffed into it. I was amazed that any notes sounded at all. The nut shells so restricted the action that some hammers couldn't even move to strike the strings. All the shells were empty, but many had been emptied through little holes in the side, that left the rest of the shell intact. The inside of the piano looked like the den of some strange type of thieves.

I went to find the owner to describe my discovery, and I asked whether he was in the habit of stashing nut shells inside his piano. He was a little set back by my question. We had a good laugh about it, and he said that no one had been near the piano for quite some time. Except for the shells, there was not much evidence around, and we wondered where such a bountiful supply of nuts could have come from. I didn't have to look far to locate the source. There was a large crockery bowl, always full of nuts, on a table in the same room as the piano. The owner and his wife each thought the other was enjoying the nuts and regularly replenished the bowl but, in fact, the chipmunks played like bandits.

I ended up cleaning the piano thoroughly, and it took the better part of the day. But, when I was finished, we were both happy that this was the piano's only problem. The owner immediately removed the bowl of nuts from his music room.

Even though this is an exceptional sticky key problem, you may come across something that you can repair by yourself if you take the time to investigate. It is, at least, worth your while to look and try to identify the problem; it may save you money. If, after a careful examination of the keys along the lines covered in the following pages, you can't find the cause of the malfunction, then you really should call a piano technician. More often than not, it will be one of the five reasons that makes a key stick or play sluggishly.

3.3 STICKY KEYS — INSTRUCTIONS

The most common complaint of pianists and piano owners in general is sticky keys. Sticky or sluggish keys are caused by a number of conditions. The first step in correcting the problem is to try to identify the cause. As you read these instructions, identify the parts as they are mentioned.

Closely examine the key that is sticking. If you find only white keys sticking and black keys working fine, the problem might be a warped *keyslip.* The keyslip is a strip of wood that runs the length of the *keybed* and protects the keys. Keyslips have a great tendency to warp. Even with new pianos, the keyslip can warp; and the result is that the white keys rub on the keyslip, are prevented from moving freely, and stick down. This is a very common problem, and it is solved the same way on both grand and vertical pianos. Insert a matchbook cover, business card, or any small piece of cardboard between the keyslip and *keyblock* at each end of the keyboard. A small piece of cardboard placed in this fashion is called a *shim.* Shims create more clearance between the keyslip and the key front and, very often, will solve the problem. If you still have sticking white keys only, the keyslip must be removed, and shims placed all along the base of the keyslip. Make sure that the shims do not interfere with the movement of the key. Refer to Plate No. 12 for exact shim placement.

Manufacturers have anticipated this common problem in many new vertical and grand pianos. To alleviate it, they have mounted *adjusting screws* (1) into the keybed (2) in order to make spacing a bit easier.

After you have removed the keyslip, check the keybed for screws of the type shown in Plate No. 13. If your piano has screws similar to those shown, you simply turn them out until the proper clearance is achieved. I recommend turning them about one-half turn and checking the key clearance. If there is not enough clearance with the keyslip attached, then remove the keyslip again, and turn them another one-half turn. Turning the screws out too much is not desirable because it can make reinstallation of the keyslip very difficult.

SHIM PLACEMENT

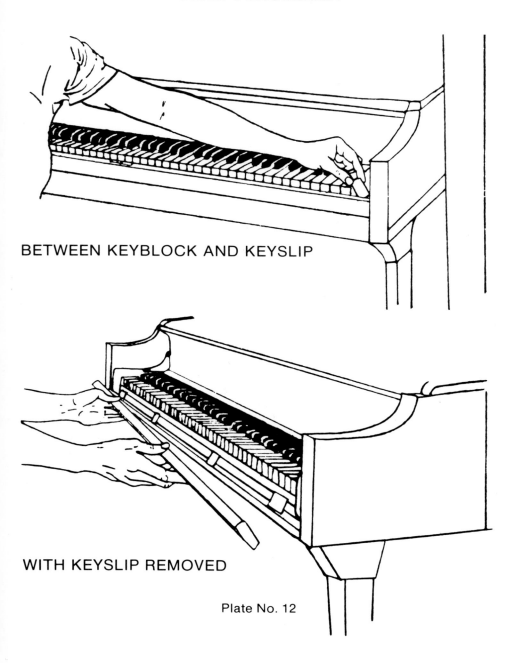

BETWEEN KEYBLOCK AND KEYSLIP

WITH KEYSLIP REMOVED

Plate No. 12

MODERN VERTICAL PIANO WITH KEYSLIP REMOVED

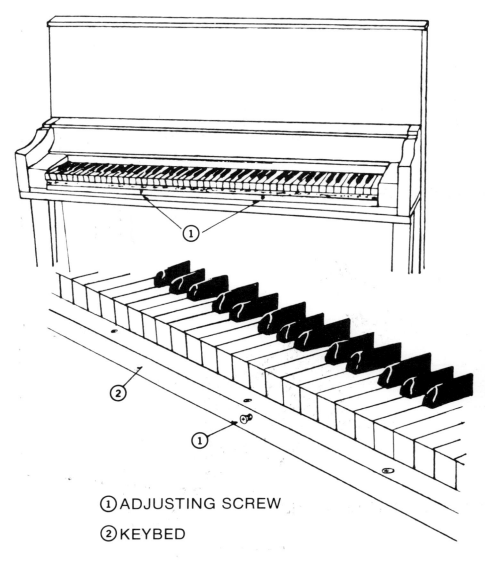

① ADJUSTING SCREW

② KEYBED

Plate No. 13

After making all the necessary adjustments, reattach the keyslip. There should be sufficient clearance for the white keys to function properly.

If the problem is not a warped keyslip, then it is time to look further. Raise the lid, and fold it back, or prop it open against the wall. It is a good idea to have a cloth between the lid and the wall to prevent damage to the piano finish. Next, remove the music shelf. Usually there are two screws (pins) that attach the music shelf to the sides of the piano. Once these are out, the music shelf should slide toward you on a track (guide pins). Slide it easily out of the piano, and set it aside.

Next, remove the fallboard. Fallboards come in a variety of different styles. As a general rule, look to determine how the fallboard is attached to the frame, and remove the screws holding it in place. Be sure to remember where all the screws came from when you put them aside.

The last part to be removed for the vertical piano preliminary inspection is the fall strip. It is usually attached by one or more nuts in the center section of the keyboard, and by two screws, one in each keyblock. Remove the screws and nut(s), and store them with the other screws. Now lift the fall strip out of the piano.

When you have removed the music shelf, fallboard, and fall strip, you have completed the most difficult part of correcting most sticky key problems. Look for the obvious. First, try to see how the piano key works. Press it down, and watch how the note plays. Notice how the key rocks on its *balance pin* (see Plate No. 14), and how close one key is to the next. By observing the movement of the piano key, you will usually be able to see whether anything like a penny or other small object has become lodged between the keys, causing sluggish response when played. Maybe a pencil has fallen into the action and is interfering with the key's ability to strike the string. These obvious foreign object problems occur occasionally and can render a key almost useless. If this is the case, just carefully remove the object, and your problem is solved. Many piano technicians have done "brilliant" repair jobs by just removing a pencil.

Piano keys are made of soft wood, usually sugar pine, which absorbs moisture easily when a piano is subjected to high humidity. This causes swelling of the wood and the *felt bushings* that surround the balance and *front rail pins,* which hold the key in place. When a key is in this condition, it is very slow to repeat and is referred to as a sluggish key. To correct this problem, you must increase the clearance between the pin and the bushing itself. You do this by squeezing the felt bushing on the key. First, you must remove the key from the piano.

41

To remove a piano key, lift up the end of the key closest to you, and gently pull the back of the key out of the piano. You will now notice that the key rides on two pins, balance (2) and front rail (3), with two separate bushings, front and back. One bushing is in the center of the key and surrounds the balance pin (see Plate No. 15), while the other is located under the area where you strike the key and surrounds the front rail pin (see Plate No. 14). Both these bushings must be opened wider to give greater clearance for the pins. To open the bushing, squeeze it with *easing pliers.* If easing pliers are not available, common needle nose pilers will do the job just fine. Be careful not to squeeze too much, as this would make the key too loose. Too much side play is not desirable.

Reinsert the key in the same manner that it was removed, and check again for sluggishness. If the bushing is still too tight, repeat the process as often as necessary. The proper clearance between bushing and pin is one that allows for unrestricted motion with as little side play as possible.

Sometimes the keys themselves become slightly warped, resulting in friction between two neighboring keys. To correct this problem, make sure that the warped key is centered as much as possible. You can bend the balance pin to align a key properly. Use a screwdriver with the palm of your hand to bend the pin. If the key is centered, but still rubs against its neighbor, remove the key, and sandpaper the contacting surfaces. Replace the key, and again check for clearance.

These are the most common solutions to the most common problem: sticky keys. If none of these suggestions works for sticky or sluggish keys, your problem may be of a more serious nature. This is the time to reassemble the piano and call a piano technician. However, most sticky key complaints that I've handled turned out to have one of the simple causes.

When reassembling the piano, start with the fall strip, next the fallboard, the music shelf, and lastly, close the lid. Work in a careful and organized manner, and you won't have any difficulties.

PIANO KEY — REMOVAL AND BUSHINGS

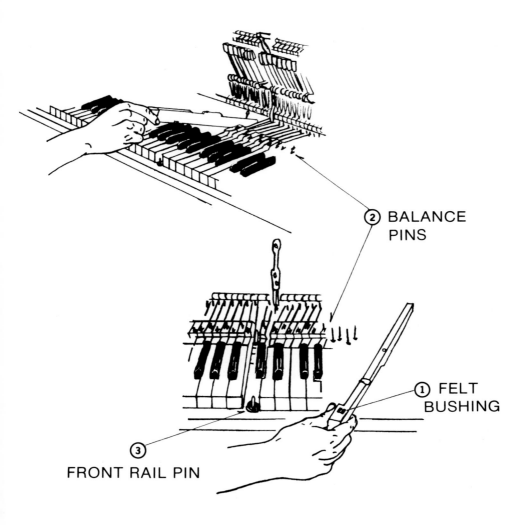

② BALANCE PINS

① FELT BUSHING

③ FRONT RAIL PIN

Plate No. 14

KEY CENTERING TECHNIQUE

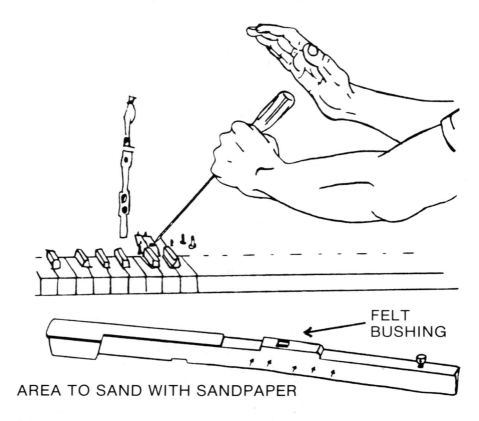

FELT BUSHING

AREA TO SAND WITH SANDPAPER

SQUEEZING (EASING) KEY BUSHING

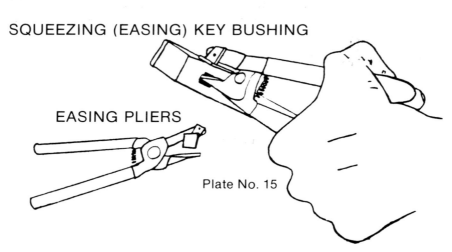

EASING PLIERS

Plate No. 15

44

3.4 STICKY KEYS — SPINET PIANO

As described in the *Piano Types* section, spinet pianos look like small console pianos but have one important difference, a drop action. The action doesn't sit on top of the keys; it rests below them. Examine the illustrations in the *Piano Types* section and in this section, and you will see what I mean.

Sticky keys on a spinet piano can originate from any one of the previously mentioned general sticky key problems, or from the particular spinet problem, the *lifter elbow.* Many spinet elbows are made of plastic, and over the years the plastic deteriorates and becomes brittle and finally breaks. When a key on a spinet piano will not play and remains in the down position, it usually has a broken elbow.

To determine whether a broken elbow is the cause, you must remove the lower frame and look inside the piano action. In the *Spinet Piano Action* illustration, there is an enlargement of the *spinet replacement elbow* (7). It can be bought very inexpensively at a piano supply store, or from your piano technician, and is very easy to install.

Carefully remove the broken elbow by crushing it with pliers; usually it will break easily.* Without removing the pin, simply snap on the replacement elbow, and screw the *lifter wire* (4) into the new elbow. Insert the lifter wire properly into the key, and the key should work just fine.

Spinet pianos are very popular and are used in many homes as practice pianos. If you study the drawing, you will notice that the action works similarly to that in most uprights. However, because it is below the keyboard rather than above it, and because the lifter wires block access to the action, spinets are difficult to repair. If any problems other than broken lifter elbows (causing a key to malfunction) occurs, it is recommended that you call a piano technician for service.

* The plastic fragments can be cleaned up later.

SPINET PIANO ACTION

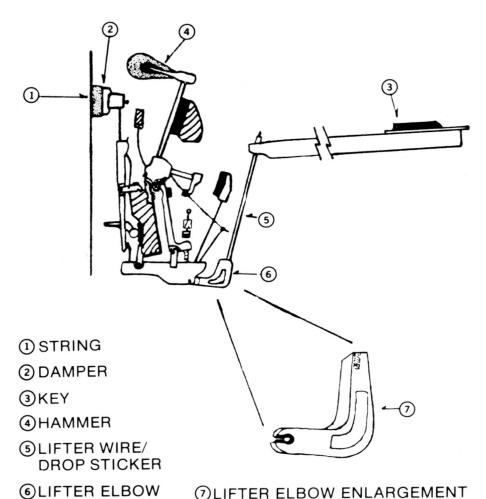

① STRING
② DAMPER
③ KEY
④ HAMMER
⑤ LIFTER WIRE/ DROP STICKER
⑥ LIFTER ELBOW

⑦ LIFTER ELBOW ENLARGEMENT
or
SPINET REPLACEMENT ELBOW

Plate No. 16

46

3.5 PEDALS — FUNCTION

In vertical pianos the pedal assembly is known as the trapwork. In grand pianos the pedal *lyre* supports the pedals. Some pianos have two pedals, but most have three.

In vertical and grand pianos the right pedal is the *sustaining pedal,* sometimes called the *loud pedal.* When it is depressed, all of the dampers are lifted at once; dampers are shown clearly in the piano action illustrations. The dampers sit on the strings preventing the strings from sounding until the note is struck. When all of the dampers are lifted at once, all of the notes played will continue to ring until the sustaining pedal is released.

The left pedal is called the *soft pedal.* In vertical pianos this pedal moves all the hammers closer to the strings. This repositioning of the hammers reduces the distance they travel and reduces their force in striking the strings. The less the striking force, the softer the resulting note.

In most grand pianos the left pedal shifts the whole keyboard and action a little to the right. The hammers strike fewer strings at once and create a softer tone. Three strings comprise a treble and middle octave note. When the action is shifted by the left pedal, only two strings are struck by the hammer. Besides being called the soft pedal, this is referred to as the *una corda* pedal.

Most quality pianos will have a third pedal. The third pedal is between the loud and the soft pedals and is called the *sostenuto pedal.* When this pedal is depressed, the notes played just before activation of the pedal will sustain (continue to ring) after the keys have been released. Any notes played after the pedal has been depressed will not sustain but will sound normally *(staccato).*

In many vertical pianos the middle pedal is used for sustaining the bass notes. When it is depressed, all the dampers rise off the strings in the bass section. The pianist can strike a chord in the bass section and play with both hands in the treble without sustaining the sound of the treble notes. This phenomenon is sometimes referred to as the *third hand effect.*

In other vertical pianos, depressing the middle pedal positions a thick strip of felt between the hammers and the strings throughout the length of the piano. This felt strip, attached to a bar hung inside the cabinet, muffles the sound on every note of the piano. If you live in an apartment or practice in an area where your playing might disturb others, this is a good pedal function to have as it allows you to practice quietly without the piano's full voice. When the third pedal has this feature, it is called the *practice pedal.*

3.6 SQUEAKY PEDALS — GRAND PIANO

Most of the annoying squeaks in a piano come from the pedal assembly. Pedals can go out of adjustment through normal use or when disassembled in moving a piano. To adjust the pedals, all you have to do is look at the setup and turn the appropriate *adjusting nut* (3) to lengthen or shorten the *connecting rod* (5).

You eliminate excess play (lost motion) in the pedal of a grand piano by turning the adjusting nut to lengthen the connecting rod. Sometimes the *leather pads* (4) create a squeak when the pedal is used. It is best to lubricate the leather surfaces with powdered graphite, not oil.

GRAND PIANO PEDAL LYRE — REAR VIEW

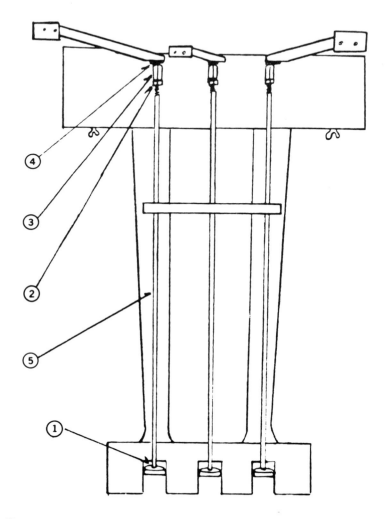

①PEDAL ④LEATHER PAD

②LOCK NUT ⑤CONNECTING ROD

③ADJUSTING NUT

Plate No. 17

3.7 SQUEAKY PEDALS — VERTICAL PIANO

Pedals on vertical pianos are adjusted in a way similar to that of grand pianos. The *adjusting nuts* (4), situated in the bottom of a vertical piano, are turned to adjust the *trap levers* (1). However, you must first remove the lower frame. It snaps off easily. Next, work the pedals to locate the squeak. If it is noticeable, apply a little oil to the metal parts that interact. This is one of the few places where oil can be used on a piano.

Sometimes the pedal *dowels* (2), which connect the trapwork to the action, squeak. Pedal dowels are usually made of wood. Through the years the wood can warp. A warped dowel rubbing against the frame of the piano causes a squeak whenever the pedal is used. The best lubricant to use in this case is soap. Just rub soap on the contacting wood surfaces and you will eliminate the squeak. If the warp in the pedal dowel is very severe and prevents the pedal's proper function, the dowel should be replaced. Replacing a pedal dowel on a vertical piano is an involved procedure and should be done by a qualified piano technician.

VERTICAL PIANO TRAPWORK

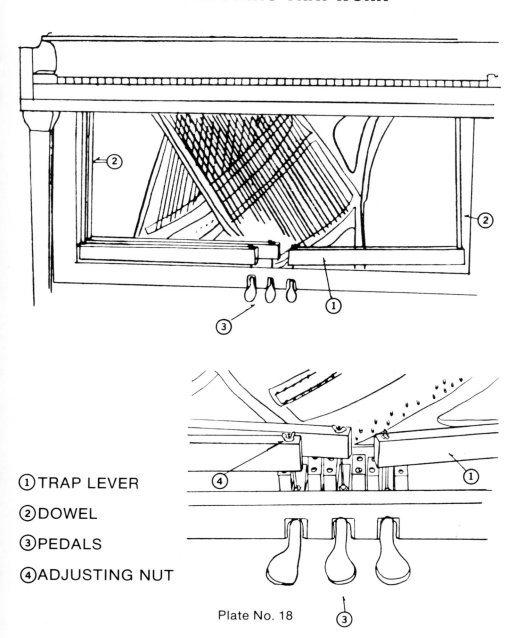

① TRAP LEVER

② DOWEL

③ PEDALS

④ ADJUSTING NUT

Plate No. 18

51

3.8 VOICING

The tonal quality of a piano can be changed by properly shaping and conditioning the hammers. Technicians call this *voicing*. Piano hammers are made of felt, pressed and glued around a wood molding. The different layers of felt on a hammer can be identified by their different colors. After the felt layers are glued and tacked to the molding, the hammers are lacquered before they are installed in the piano. Lacquering hardens and conditions the felt.

New piano hammers are conditioned to what I call the down side of neutral. This conditioning leaves the hammers softer than is desirable for full piano tone. As a new piano is played the hammer felts compress, causing the piano's tone to become more brilliant. Exactly how much new hammers will compress cannot be anticipated because each piano is unique.

After the first few months of constant use the hammers settle and no longer compress. As the piano is played the hammers begin to retain the impression of the strings they strike. This is the time to have your piano voiced to your own particular needs. Many contemporary artists prefer a very brilliant tone while most classical artists enjoy a rich, mellow tonal quality. No matter what your musical tastes, voicing will make the piano's tone cleaner and more dynamic. If the hammers are not voiced, the strings will cut through the soft hammer felt and the hammers will deteriorate much more rapidly than necessary.

There are three basic steps to voicing a piano. First, the hammers are filed and shaped with sandpaper. This creates properly curved surfaces to strike the strings when the piano is played. Correct hammer curvature helps to prevent string breakage. Next, the hammers are lacquered and dried. Properly hardening them brightens the piano's tone and at the same time conditions, preserves, and protects the hammers from premature wear. The last step is the most delicate. The hammers are repeatedly pierced or needled with a voicing tool. This is done to refine and even the piano's tone.

Most pianos should be voiced when the hammers show excessive wear. Pianos used for performances and in studios require voicing much more often than pianos in homes. A dull, lifeless tone is an indication that a piano needs to be voiced. Voicing will dramatically enhance a piano's tone and increase your enjoyment of its sound.

4

Why Does A Piano Need To Be Tuned?

4.1 STRINGS — GENERAL

A piano is a string instrument. The strings are made of steel and are under considerable tension. Most pianos have about two hundred to two hundred thirty-five strings, and each string exerts a tension of about one hundred sixty-five pounds on the average. This translates to around eighteen tons of string tension throughout an average size piano. A nine foot concert grand piano supports about thirty tons of string tension.

The lowest eight strings of the bass section in a modern concert grand are single. This means that there is only one string for each note (key). The next twelve notes have pairs of strings, two strings for each key. All the rest of the notes have three strings each. When a key is played in the middle and treble sections, the hammer hits three strings simultaneously. Piano dampers prevent the note from ringing after release of the key. However, the top twenty-one keys have no dampers because their vibrations are so small that it is not necessary to stop them.

String diameters vary greatly in a piano. The deepest bass copper-wound string is approximately one-third of an inch in diameter (including the copper winding). The highest steel strings of a piano are about one-thirtieth of an inch in diameter. As can be imagined, strings are always trying to pull back to their original relaxed state. A piano takes anywhere from two to five years of constant string tension at concert pitch to "settle" and to be able to hold a tune for any length of time.

The illustration of a *Concert Grand* shows the positions of the basic piano parts. A concert grand piano is just under nine feet long (some concert grands are even longer). The piano case or frame (1) encloses the plate (2), soundboard (3), pinblock, bridges (4), and tuning pins (5). All of these basic parts serve to support the strings (6). If any of these basic parts change position, the tension of the strings changes, and the piano goes out of tune.

A piano's plate is made of cast iron and is usually painted a brass color. The plate supports much of the string tension while it exerts a force that helps preserve the crown or curvature of the soundboard. The pinblock is located under the plate and has the tuning pins driven into it. The pinblock is made of laminated wood for superior strength. The piano strings are wound around the tuning pins. When a tuner tunes a piano, he generally increases the tension on the strings by turning the threaded tuning pins tighter. Ideally, pianos should be tuned to concert pitch, commonly accepted as A440 (which means that A above middle C on the keyboard should vibrate at 440 cycles per second).

CONCERT GRAND

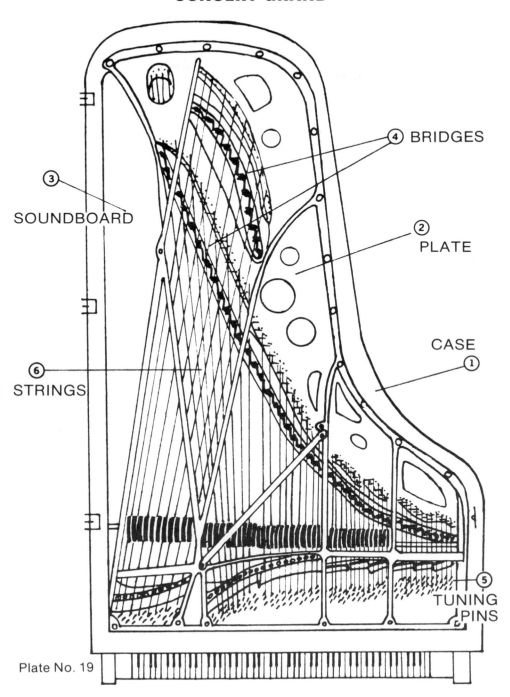

④ BRIDGES

③ SOUNDBOARD

② PLATE

① CASE

⑥ STRINGS

⑤ TUNING PINS

Plate No. 19

If you don't have your piano tuned regularly, you are neglecting an extremely sensitive, not to mention expensive, instrument. The value of your piano decreases accordingly. If you decide to have your piano tuned after many years, a very knowledgeable tuner is required. Much damage can be done to a piano that hasn't been tuned regularly and if the tuner tries to pull it up to pitch incorrectly. The biggest danger is cracking the plate, which is a very serious problem. A qualified tuner approaches a neglected piano with caution.

A neglected piano must be brought up to concert pitch gradually (which could mean a double tuning the first time), and then repeatedly tuned to stabilize the string tension. Four or more tunings may be necessary to stabilize a neglected piano or a new piano. A piano should be stabilized within a four week period so that it will hold its tune for a few months. In other words, a piano may require as much as a tuning per week to stabilize it at concert pitch if it is new or has been neglected. Since this can run into costly tuning bills, it pays to keep your piano in good tune throughout its useful life.

4.2 STRINGS — STRETCH

Strings in new pianos stretch out of tune very rapidly. They lose their tension and go flat owing to their elasticity. The problem is similar in old pianos that have to be raised one-quarter to one-half tone to bring them to concert pitch. As soon as they are tuned, they immediately begin stretching flat. The tuner then must re-tune the piano to stress the strings properly.

After the first five years of a piano's life, its steel strings begin to "settle" if it has been tuned regularly. Then a six month or yearly tuning schedule will suffice for most pianos. If the piano has been neglected for the first five years of its existence and has only been tuned once or twice, it can settle as much as a half tone low. This means that when the note C is played the note B is produced. Practicing on a piano in this condition is especially harmful to the ears of young people starting piano lessons. It is important to train the ear at an early age so that the beginner can develop a true perspective of "relative pitch." A properly trained ear serves as the basic building block for many professional musicians.

The piano is designed to be tuned at concert pitch; this is the pitch at which the piano will sound its best. Maximum life will result for the instrument if concert pitch is maintained. New strings are always stretching flat and require regular adjustment. When properly maintained strings have settled, the amount of adjustment needed decreases. The tuning pins may only have to be turned a small fraction in order to bring the piano to concert pitch. Consequently, less frequent tunings are necessary.

4.3 PINBLOCK

The superior strength of a laminated pinblock derives from its construction as well as its lamination. Slabs of wood are glued together with their grains running at different angles. A pinblock formed in this manner supports the tuning pins without cracking and creates the right amount of grip so that the tuning pins are tight but also loose enough to be turned smoothly when the piano is tuned.

The pinblock is glued to the soundboard and to the piano case and also attached under the plate by large screws. It is important for a pinblock to make solid contact with the entire area of the plate. If part of it touches the plate and part does not, uneven string tension results. A piano with uneven string tension will not hold a tune.

The *Hardwood Pinblock* illustration shows the string (1) attached to the tuning pin (2), which is driven deep into the pinblock. The string's tension is absorbed by the tuning pin. This gives you an idea of the strain to which a pinblock is subjected. The piano plate covers the entire pinblock but has been left out of the picture.

The illustration in Section 1.5 shows how the pinblock is set in the piano with reference to the piano action and plate.

HARDWOOD PINBLOCK

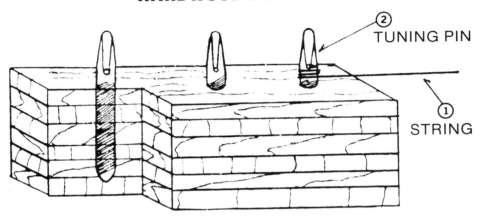

② TUNING PIN

① STRING

Plate No. 20

4.4 PLAYING

When a key is struck, the hammer pounds on the strings and quickly releases to the "checked," or rest, position. The more force exerted on a piano when it is played, the faster the loss of tune. Pounding will knock the strings out of tune on old and new pianos alike. However, if the piano has been maintained properly and if its strings have settled, it will withstand forceful playing and stay in tune relatively well.

More often than not, a piano tuner waits in the wings (offstage) at a professional pianist's concert. During intermission the tuner re-tunes the piano and prepares it for the next part of the performance. Concert artists use such force when playing that few pianos will hold a tune satisfactorily. This should give you an idea of how quickly forceful playing can make a piano lose its tune and also of why concert artists' pianos need tuning more often than others.

4.5   TUNING PINS

A tuning pin has a hole in its top portion and very fine threads on its bottom portion. The hole is for a piano string to be inserted, and the threads help the pin keep a tight grip when installed into the pinblock. First a hole is drilled through the plate and into the pinblock, and then the tuning pin is hammered into this hole. The threaded portion of the tuning pin creates added friction in the pinblock to aid in keeping the pin tight.

Most newer pianos have tight tuning pins, and sometimes you can hear the pins "crack" in the pinblock as they are turned, in testimony to their tightness. When temperature and humidity affect the pinblock, the pins gradually loosen. Constant string tension pulling on them also contributes to their losing their grip. When a tuner tells you that your piano has loose or slipping pins, he means that the tuning pins do not hold securely against the string tension. They either "skip" or turn rapidly. Loose pins are normal occurrences in many older pianos.

The best cure for loose pins is replacement with new pins one size larger. This means re-stringing and re-pinning a piano, a major repair. Before re-pinning, I usually try to find an easier and less expensive solution. The technician can try to drive the tuning pins further into the pinblock by hammering them down with a tuning pin *setter.* If this does not tighten them enough to hold a tune, he can treat the pinblock itself with a chemical solution. When droppered into the space around a tuning pin's base in the pinblock, the solution causes the wood to swell around the pin, forming a tighter fit between pin and pinblock. The solution should be applied at least three times and allowed to dry completely (which takes a day or so) between applications.

If both these simple remedies are ineffective, then complete re-stringing and re-pinning are recommended. Many tuners will not try the alternatives and will immediately urge re-pinning. However, these simple remedies are often very effective. In fact, they work most of the time and can last for years, depending on your piano. As a piano owner, you should be aware of them and be sure to ask about them before agreeing to a major repair job.

4.6   HUMIDITY AND TEMPERATURE

As pointed out previously, humidity and temperature affect all of the piano's parts. Extreme dampness and excessive heat are a piano's greatest enemies. In terms of a piano's tune, the part most affected by humidity and temperature is the soundboard. Although heavily coated with a protective varnish, the soundboard is still vulnerable to seasonal changes.

In spring the additional humidity in the air is absorbed by the wood in the piano. As moisture settles into the soundboard, its crown increases, creating more tension on the plate and strings, and the piano goes sharp in pitch. Conversely, in winter, with the drying heat of warmed rooms, the crown gradually decreases, and the piano goes flat in pitch. This increase in spring and decrease in winter is known as *seasonal pitch change.*

Humidity is much more significant for a piano's tune than temperature. Nevertheless, both change seasonally, and both affect pitch.

4.7   EXPERT TUNING

A piano should be tuned by an expert. Many devices and many piano modifications have been designed to assist the piano owner in tuning his own instrument, but none have been successful. A novice cannot tune properly, and a novice can damage a piano.

In 1800 a piano builder named Hawkins developed mechanical wrest-pins that permitted tuning by varying pressure on piano pins. Other designers installed additional bridges in pianos to facilitate tuning. John Geib patented a buff stop to silence one string while another was being tuned. Streicher and Stein went one step further and modified the una corda pedal to mute selected strings so that other strings could be tuned. John J. Wise of Baltimore in 1833 invented a gadget that indicated the number of string vibrations on a dial. Despite these attempts to aid the amateur, the job of tuning a piano remained in the hands of professionals trained in the art.

Another approach to solving the tuning problem was the single string or *unichord* piano, produced by Pleyel and Stanhope, prosperous manufacturers of conventional pianos. After numerous experiments, they gave up on their idea because its sound was unsatisfactory when compared to a full size instrument.

Other piano builders suggested eliminating piano strings altogether! However, when you remove the piano strings, you no longer have an acoustic piano — a bit like cutting off your nose to spite your face. They developed an array of odd instruments that could be tuned by means of springs attached to metal tongues, adjustable metal rods used to produce the tones, and other revolutionary configurations. Such pianos became the forerunners of the electronic pianos used so much today: but even these instruments need to be tuned by technicians trained in electronic pianos. Although the manufacturers' search for an owner-tunable piano did establish a new class of instrument, it did not change the acoustic piano, which still has a complex string arrangement and which still should be tuned by an expert.

A piano tuned by an expert will sound better and last longer than a piano tuned by a novice. The expert knows how to "set" a pin by pulling it slightly above the correct pitch and letting the string stretch back just the right amount, so that the note "settles" at exactly correct pitch. A note played hard by a concert pianist stays in tune longer if it has been "set". Many piano tuners are adept at this technique, which is just one of the differences between a good tuning and a mediocre tuning.

Quality tuning is an important factor in piano maintenance. All pianists, no matter what their level of accomplishment, enjoy the sound of a properly tuned piano. An old master tuner I studied under said that an unskilled tuner could make his customers believe their pianos were in tune until those customers heard the sound of an expertly tuned piano. My teacher encouraged me to strive for perfection with every piano I tuned. He said that striving for perfection would ensure that my tuning would become better and better and that, as a result, my clientele would grow through the years. I owe much to this great teacher's advice, and I try to follow it every day.

Make every effort to find a piano tuner who is interested in giving you the most professional service available, and who cares about what he does. This is the tuner to contract for the job of maintaining your piano.

4.8 HOW OFTEN SHOULD A PIANO BE TUNED?

A piano should be tuned as often as necessary. This depends entirely on the individual situation. If a piano is used as a piece of furniture and is rarely played, it should be tuned only once a year. If it is in a recording studio and is played every day, it should be tuned daily.

Pianos in homes have less stringent requirements than pianos in studios. The most extreme case for in-home tuning is a new piano, or one that has recently been pulled up one-quarter tone or more. Such an instrument needs tuning at least four times within the first twelve months to ensure that it remains at concert pitch and to give the strings a chance to settle correctly. After the first year, and for the next few years, it should be tuned every four to six months. Then it should be tuned according to its use. Generally, if a piano is used daily and is in good condition, tuning every four to six months should keep it in top form and in concert pitch.

During the summer months in the United States, there are many fine music camps for outstanding students who want to sharpen their musical skills. These camps provide instruction in all musical instruments as well as in band and orchestra. It is difficult for the camps to furnish enough pianos for two main reasons. First is the initial cost of pianos. Second is that camp buildings are generally constructed for summer use, three months at most, and not insulated as well as buildings intended for year-round use. It is not wise to leave pianos in such surroundings, but pianos are difficult to move. Most summer camps, therefore, do not invest in many pianos for their students. At best, they have only a few pianos, which can mean that students are severely curtailed in practice time.

One of the finest music camps in the country made a commitment to its piano students to provide enough pianos for practice. In fact, the camp started out as simply a teacher with a few piano students. Because it offered an adequate number of pianos both for practice and for concerts, it grew to be a respected music camp visited by outstanding musicians. There were gifted piano students from high school, colleges, and post-college levels. The piano teachers were carefully selected, and an attempt was made to match students and teachers in a manner calculated to bring out the students' best efforts.

The music camp was located close enough to Tanglewood, Massachusetts, the summer home of the Boston Symphony Orchestra, to permit some of the greatest artists who performed at Tanglewood to drop in at the camp. The artists would counsel students and give performances for the many music lovers who attended the camp's weekly concerts.

My father, the tuner-technician for the camp, followed a program to tune and repair each piano at the beginning of the season. The concert grand used in the weekly performances was tuned and maintained every week. It was a fine old grand that had been rebuilt several years before, and great care was given to its protection. It was kept locked except during practice for concerts and, of course, during concerts themselves. When not in use, it was covered with heavy pads to protect it as much as possible from summer temperatures and humidity. However, age and the New England winters combined to take their toll on the piano, and its tuning pins were no longer as tight and secure as they should have been. The instrument needed constant servicing to keep its tune for performances, and even then it was touch and go.

A great American pianist was scheduled to appear at the camp one particular summer. He had chosen a Beethoven piece written expressly to demonstrate the capabilities of a piano's eighty-eight keys. The camp's old grand was tuned the day of the performance. Surprisingly, it held its tune quite well except for one note near the top of the treble section.

In the treble section of a piano, each note has three strings, each of which must be tuned exactly the same as the other two to produce a clear sound. Unfortunately, the note that didn't hold its tune was one that Beethoven liked and used constantly as the accentuating high note throughout the piece. Every time the artist hit the note, a resounding discord rang out. The highly trained musical audience did get to know when to expect that discord, and laboriously prepared for it each time, while my father cringed.

My sister was a piano student at the camp that summer, and we all remember the concert with a bit of humor. My father, being the camp's tuner, felt terrible and to this day shudders when we laugh about the incident. The artist was very philosophic about it. Perhaps one of the marks of great pianists is that they understand the precarious art of piano tuning better than most.

5

How To Protect
Your Investment

5.1 HUMIDIFIER / DEHUMIDIFIER

Climate can have serious effects on a piano. If a piano is moved from a very wet climate to a very dry climate, the wood and other parts will start to split and fall apart. It may be difficult to control the climate outside the piano, but it is easy to control the climate within the piano if you need to. I recommend a climate control system only if your piano is in an area where extreme changes in humidity exist. For example, if the piano is near the beach or in the desert, a climate control device is necessary.

In a very wet environment, unless controlled, moist air will rust the steel parts in the piano and warp the wood. To evaporate moisture within the piano, a *heater bar* (dehumidifier) can be very effective. It can be purchased from your piano technician or from a piano store and is usually not too expensive. The heater bar is placed inside a vertical piano or underneath a grand piano. But there are other solutions.

One of my clients has a console piano in her beach house. Harsh, moist salt air attacks pianos kept in beach homes within a very short time and I always expect to find broken strings and similar rust related problems when I service these instruments. However, from the first day I serviced this client's piano I noticed there was no rust damage, no broken strings, and no heater bar. I examined the piano carefully and found that in spite of years of being on the beach, the piano's strings were as shiny as the day the piano was bought. Her secret was a little bag of white flour that she hung inside the piano and changed every few months. Judging from what I've seen, this practice is a good, practical way to keep a vertical piano moisture free. However in the long run, knowing how prices are today, I wonder which is more economical; the one time cost of the heater bar or the continuing cost of the flour?

On the other hand, in a very dry environment, a *humidifier* (a small reservoir with a heater bar and pads in it) should be placed inside a vertical piano or attached underneath a grand piano. When the air becomes too dry, the bar heats the water inside the bucket and provides the moisture needed to protect the piano. A humidifier can also be purchased from your piano technician or from a piano store.

If you live in an area of drastic climate changes, very humid to very dry, I recommend a complete climate control system. It consists of a humidifier, dehumidifier, and *humidistat* control. The climate control system is self-regulating; it uses household current as its source of electrical power. A system like this gives your piano the ultimate in climate protection and works effectively and reliably for years.

PIANO CLIMATE CONTROL SYSTEM

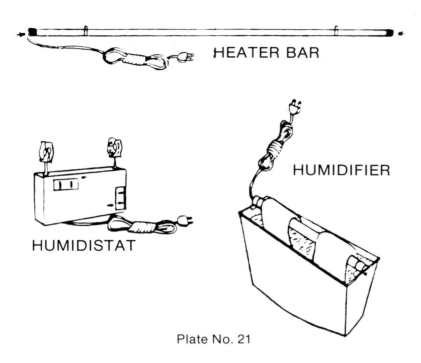

HEATER BAR

HUMIDIFIER

HUMIDISTAT

Plate No. 21

5.2 MOTH PROTECTION

Moths are a very common problem in pianos. They lay their eggs in dust that accumulates in piano hammers and bushings, which are made of felt. When the moth eggs hatch, the larvae eat the felt. The best moth protection is to keep your piano clean. Cleaning is essential in order to protect pianos from damage. I recommend a complete piano cleaning once a year. However, if you already have moths, you can do a few things to eliminate the pests.

There is a spray for demothing a piano, specifically made for piano felts, which can be purchased at a piano supply store or from your technician. Apply the spray directly to the action and hammers. As a temporary treatment to demoth a piano, mothballs can be used. However, try not to use mothballs that contain DDT, because the fumes from mothballs with DDT contain an acid that will rust the metal parts in the piano.

Once you have demothed your piano, keep it dust-free and you will keep it moth-free.

5.3   WHERE TO PLACE THE PIANO IN THE HOME

Piano placement is a concern of most piano owners. You should observe a few basic rules when deciding where to place your piano in your home.

Do not place the piano near a window or against an outside wall. Either of these sites provides too little protection from sunlight and climate changes. It is also not advisable to place the piano near a radiator, stove, or steam pipes. The heat will ruin the piano in winter months by drying out the glue used in the case and action. Do not place the piano on a concrete floor or near a cinderblock wall because these retain dampness.

Pianos are sensitive to their environments. A little thought to its location will help to protect your piano for years to come.

For grand pianos, in addition to thoughtful location, it is also good planning to have a table of some kind near. It is a temptation to put drinks, candles, lamps, or breakable china on the flat surfaces on either side of the music desk. But you should be aware that the music desk is not a sturdy surface. When each note is played the music desk vibrates ever so slightly, but just enough to move most objects gradually off its surface.

Many restaurant pianos are needlessly ruined by spilled drinks that were placed beside the music desk. The drink falls onto the pins, piano action, damper felts, soundboard, and other delicate parts. One restaurant piano had all of its felts eaten by ants after a sugary drink spilled off the music desk. Needless to say, repairing major damage like this was costly.

A good way to avoid the temptation to place objects on the music desk is to have a coffee table beside the piano for drinks, lamps, pictures, etc. The piano is a wonderful piece of furniture but it also is a vibrant, alive musical instrument that is not designed to support anything other than music.

5.4   A PIANO'S WORTH

On the Southern Californian coast in the mid 1970s, the piano market was full of late nineteenth century vertical pianos that had been shipped from England. Built in extraordinarily beautiful cases of fine wood and ornately crafted, these pianos were about one hundred years old when they arrived.

These old English pianos, with so-called "bird-cage" actions, have internal parts of different sizes from those of pianos built today. This makes their part replacement very difficult and their servicing financially impractical. Tuning pianos with bird cage actions is a complicated chore requiring far more time and effort than a tuner can give without charging a tremendous amount of money. He must remove the dampers to tune this style piano, which means that the notes won't stop ringing when played. Therefore he is forced to "chip" or pluck the strings when tuning.

Many tuners and technicians refused to service these instruments, and the pianos quickly went from piano stores to antique stores for sale to the general public. Unfortunately, a number of people looking for bargains purchased these old pianos. Many of them unknowingly bought a nice piece of furniture that was totally useless as a musical instrument. One such person called me to service his old English piano. We came to the conclusion that it would be far less expensive for him to rent a piano for his daughter's lessons than to try to rebuild the piano he owned. At least his daughter would have a quality instrument to play and one that would be much cheaper to maintain.

When judging a piano's worth, look at the inside as well as the outside of the case. See whether the tuning pins are tight and whether the hammers look good, and check to be sure that all of the notes function properly. Remember that a piano is valued by appearance *and* function. It is truly unfortunate when unsuspecting parents buy a piano for their children to learn on and the piano has one problem after another. Constantly needed repairs destroy the child's will to learn and drain the parents' pocketbook. It is better to buy a quality instrument for your initial investment and enjoy years of trouble free music than to buy a "bargain" and suffer years of dissatisfaction.

In the last analysis, however, whenever possible, the piano player is the one who should make the final decision on what piano to purchase. Two pianos can be built by the same piano manufacturer, on the same day, with the same style and materials, and look exactly alike, but sound completely different because each one is unique. Pianos can differ subtly, and yet profoundly. This is the nature of the instrument. Piano purchasing is a highly personal venture because what appeals to one individual may not appeal to another. So listen and be sure.

Now that you know more about pianos and how they function, don't be afraid to look at the action and the strings; pay careful attention to the tone, and decide exactly what you want. In this way, you will become a more educated consumer, and you will be happy with your rather expensive purchase. It could be your one piano purchase for a lifetime.

If you have your piano tuned and checked regularly before problems develop, its value will increase as the years go by. A properly tuned and maintained piano can be a source of great joy and many hours of fulfillment. The piano is a combination of steel, wood, iron, brass, plastic, and felt forming one of the most beautiful and sensitive instruments ever conceived.

Enjoy your piano, discover its true value, and protect it from the environment. It cost a substantial amount of money to acquire a piano in the first place. It makes good sense to do everything you can to preserve your investment.

Many old upright pianos survived generations in the same family, in the same house, and often in the same room, only to deteriorate majestically. The piano was never used. Life passed it by until finally a decision was made to junk the old beast. Eventually, the piano was hauled away to the closest dump where it was shattered into little pieces, never to be seen again. All too often, this sad end to an old upright was a normal occurrence, resulting in more pianos ending up at the dump than were being rebuilt.

Today things are a bit different. People are learning that the old upright pianos have a sound and tone quality not easily found in the newer, smaller instruments manufactured now.

One of the things our family does is to look for fine pianos and bring them into our shop for rebuilding or reconditioning. We usually have several around, awaiting their face-lifting. One that we had was a beautiful quarter-grained oak piano, not quite as tall as the very tallest upright. This piano received special attention. Upon completion, it sold immediately, and there were several potential buyers who were disappointed at missing the opportunity to purchase this fine instrument.

At the same time, over in the corner of the shop was a large, horribly painted piano, which always seemed to be in the way and was always being moved to make room for some other piano. It was an ex-player piano without the player mechanism, and with a lot of carved designs in the wood. The legs were extensively carved. Anyone who knows about furniture refinishing recognizes how hard it is to remove paint from carved wood. The fact remained that, before a new finish could be put on, the old one had to come off. Finally, just to get it out of the shop, we began work on this piano.

Indeed, refinishing it was no small job, but it was immensely rewarding. To our great amazement, under the awful, ugly paint was a beautiful mahogany wood that had very appealing markings and that refinished beautifully with clear varnish. The inside of the piano was completely reconditioned. Work there proved to be just as rewarding. The resulting tone was rich and beautiful, comparable to that of a good-sized grand piano. If there is an old upright piano in your family, maybe it isn't really an old beast. Who knows?

Some things turn out well, but sometimes results are less than satisfying. In the early days, when my father was just becoming known for rebuilding and reconditioning pianos, he answered an ad for a grand piano that someone wanted to sell. It was in a barn and had the remnants of a player mechanism in it. Mice, squirrels, and other rodents had made their homes in the player action and throughout the piano; their little skeletons were everywhere. The odor of dead things and animal waste was overwhelming. However, the price was right, and the piano was taken to our shop. Everything inside the piano was so dirty and smelly that we just removed the player mechanism and hauled it off to the dump.

Several months later, while talking to a friend who repairs and restores player pianos, my father learned that that old player was, in fact, a vintage reproducer. A reproducer not only strikes the notes, as any player does, but provides shading in tone as well. (A reproducer is to a player as a Rembrandt is to a paint by-numbers kit.) It is said that once a reproducing grand was played behind a screen at Carnegie Hall and that the audience thought for certain that a person was playing. We had thrown away thousands of dollars in irreplaceable reproducer mechanisms. Live and learn. We felt bad, it's true, but the real loser in this story was the original owner, who had no idea of the value of the instrument rotting away in his barn.

By following the recommendations for the care and maintenance of your piano, you will safeguard your investment as much as is humanly possible. However, owing to events beyond your control, perhaps you have no space along an inside wall to place the piano in your home. Perhaps your family spends part of the year in one house and part in another, leaving the piano, or two pianos if there is one at each location, alone and unattended for an extended period of time.

Necessity may dictate unfavorable conditions for a piano, but the desire to have a piano at all is sometimes overriding, even when it is known that proper care cannot be given to it. In a situation like this, it must be understood that the piano will be subjected to factors of environment that will affect it adversely. It is amazing, nevertheless, how well a piano can withstand unfavorable treatment and conditions without being relegated to uselessness. So simply do the best that you can as far as protection is concerned. Whatever the circumstances, the most important thing is to enjoy your piano.

Glossary

BALANCE PIN — pin located in the center of the piano key, also called balance rail pin

BOTTOM BOARD — supports the trapwork on the bottom of a vertical piano

BRIDGE — long, irregular shaped piece of wood attached to the soundboard that keeps the strings in proper position and helps to transmit string vibrations

BRIDLE STRAP — cloth tape that aids in the hammer's return on vertical pianos

CLIMATE CONTROL SYSTEM — dehumidifier, humidifier, and humidistat designed to control the proper humidity within the piano

CONSOLE PIANO — vertical piano forty to forty-nine inches tall and has the piano action located directly on top of the piano keys, sometimes referred to as the studio upright

CROWN — gradual curvature of the soundboard

DAMPER — piece of felt that allows the note to vibrate when lifted off the string

DROP ACTION — term used for the spinet piano action, which is located below the piano keys

DROP STICKER — spinet piano part that connects the piano keys to lifter elbows, also called lifter wires

DOWELS — parts of the trapwork that connect the trap levers to the vertical piano's action

EASING PLIERS — pliers specifically designed to squeeze piano key bushings

ESCAPEMENT — general term for the action parts that aid in hammer return

FALLBOARD — that part of the piano case that covers and protects the piano keys when the piano is not in use

FALL STRIP — a long narrow piece of wood extending the length of the piano, located between the piano keys and the fallboard, also called drop rail

FRONT RAIL PIN — pin located under the playing surface of the piano key

GRAND PIANO — piano with strings in a horizontal position

HAMMER — that part of the piano action assembly made of felt, glued and tacked to a wood molding, which strikes the string when a note is played

HAMMER BUTT — base onto which vertical piano hammers are attached

JACK — L-shaped part of a vertical piano's action that pushes the hammer toward the string when a note is played

JACK SPRING — spring attached to the base of the jack to aid in the hammer's return after a note is sounded

KEY BED — frame onto which the piano keys and action are mounted

KEYBLOCK — rectangular block of wood located at each end of the keyboard

KEYBOARD — the piano's keys

KEY BUSHING — felt padding discreetly glued to the piano key, protects the key from front rail pin and balance pin abrasion

KEYS — solid pieces of soft wood whose striking surfaces are covered with plastic or ivory

LID — moveable top cover of the piano case

LIFTER ELBOW — connects drop stickers (lifter wires) to the wippen in spinet pianos

LOWER FRAME — visible board forming the bottom face of a vertical piano case

LYRE — supports the pedals on a grand piano

MUSIC DESK — area above the keyboard for holding music

MUSIC SHELF — the part of a vertical piano case that supports the music desk

PIANO ACTION — piano mechanism that transfers the striking force from the keys to the strings when a note is played

PIANO CASE — exterior body of the piano, also called the piano frame

PINBLOCK — laminated hardwood block attached underneath the plate to hold the tuning pins in position

PLATE — also called harp, made of cast iron and serves as the primary support for the strings

PRACTICE PEDAL — center pedal on vertical pianos, when held down, it positions a thick felt strip between the hammers and the strings which reduces the piano's volume significantly

SEASONAL PITCH CHANGE — piano's general pitch variance; higher in spring and lower in winter

SOFT PEDAL — left pedal on grand and vertical pianos
    grand piano — shifts entire action a little to the right causing the treble hammers to strike only two strings per note, also called the una corda pedal
    vertical piano — moves all the hammers closer to the strings, reducing hammer travel and force when striking the strings

SOSTENUTO PEDAL — center pedal on most grand and vertical pianos
    grand piano — sustains the notes that are played just before and while the pedal is depressed
    vertical piano — sustains all the bass notes when depressed

SOUNDBOARD — large board that forms the back of a vertical piano or the bottom of a grand piano; (it) vibrates when the notes are played and amplifies the sound of the strings

SOUNDBOARD STEEL — flat piece of spring steel with a hole in one end, used in cleaning grand piano soundboards

SPINET PIANO — smallest of the vertical pianos, less than forty inches tall, has the action located below key level

SPINET REPLACEMENT ELBOW — plastic or wood lifter elbow designed for easy replacement on spinet pianos

STICKERS — part of the upright piano action that rests on the piano keys and attaches to the action

STRINGS — piano wire which is wrapped around the tuning pin and the plate, produces sound when struck by the hammers; also called music wire

SUPPORT BLOCK — supports the action in a spinet piano

SUSTAINING PEDAL — the right-most pedal on grand and vertical pianos, raises all of the dampers off the strings when held down; also called the loud pedal

TRAP LEVERS — those parts of a vertical piano trapwork that connect the pedals to the dowels

TRAPWORK — general term for the complete pedal assembly

TUNING PINS — threaded steel pins driven into the pinblock which maintain the strings' tension

TUNING PIN SETTER — tool designed to hold the tuning pin in place while the pin is hammered deeper into the pinblock; used to remedy loose or slipping tuning pins

UPRIGHT PIANO — tallest of the vertical pianos, fifty inches or more, has the piano action located above the keys

UNICHORD PIANO — piano with one string for each note

VERTICAL PIANO — piano with strings in a vertical position

VOICING — treating a piano's hammers to enhance its tone

WIPPEN — the part of a piano action that transfers the striking force from the key to the hammer

PIANO SERVICE SCHEDULE

PIANO
MANUFACTURER _____

PIANO
SERIAL NUMBER _____

DATE
MANUFACTURED _____

PIANO FINISH _____

ACTION TYPE _____

TUNING, MAINTENANCE, AND CLEANING

Date Serviced	Work Done	Technician's Name & Phone	Next Service Due

Date Serviced	Work Done	Technician's Name & Phone	Next Service Due

Date Serviced	Work Done	Technician's Name & Phone	Next Service Due